Reframing the Latino Immigration Debate

REFRAMING THE LATINO IMMIGRATION DEBATE
Towards a Humanistic Paradigm

ALVARO HUERTA

Photography by Antonio Turok

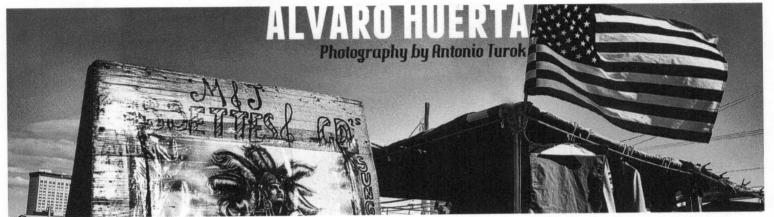

San Diego State University Press ~ 2013

Reframing the Latino Immigration Debate: Towards a Humanistic Paradigm by Alvaro Huerta is published by San Diego State University Press.

San Diego State University Press publications may be purchased at discount for educational, business, or sales promotional use. For information write SDSU Press Next Generation Publishing Initiative (NGPI), San Diego, California 92182-6020.

All photographs by Antonio Turok except as noted.

Book Design by Guillermo Nericcio García, for *memogr@phics designcasa*, memo@sdsu.edu

ISBN-13 978-1-938537-03-5
ISBN-10 1938537033

http://sdsupress.sdsu.edu
http://hype.sdsu.edu

FIRST EDITION

Printed in the United States of America

Immigrants Living in Trailer, New Mexico, 2001

The dreamer is the designer of tomorrow...
Suppress the dreamer, and the world
will deteriorate towards barbarism.

— *Ricardo Flores Magón*
Partido Liberal Mexicano, 1921

Contents

Dedications

To Catalina, Soledad, Ofelia, Salomón Jr., Rosa,
Noel, Ismael, and the rest of the Huerta and Mejia
clans—both here and in Mexico.

I especially dedicate this book to my wife, Antonia
—a wise and beautiful Chicana—whom I love dearly.
I couldn't have completed this book without her
inspiration and unconditional support.

Finally, with this book, Antonia and I aim to inspire
Joaquin to reach his full potential and pursue his dreams.

(Photograph by unknown, Mexico, 1954)

In Memoriam
Salomón Chavez Huerta (1930 – 1996)
& Carmen Mejia Huerta (1939 – 2011)

Foreword

JUAN GÓMEZ-QUIÑONES

Dr. Alvaro Huerta knows of hard lives and anguished dreams that drive immigrants to come to this country. Experience is his first prerequisite for writing about immigrants whose lives he has shared. His second is his deep practice of broad and detailed study of immigrants and the immigrant-driven political economy surrounding all of us. The public policy pertinent to both lives and statistics he has long ago concluded needs reformulation premised on the good of immigrants being the yardstick. He deplores the expedient rhetorical ploys by politicians to satisfy the anti-immigrant audiences.

Dr. Huerta makes several references to the immigration history of Latinos in the United States. First and foremost is that Latino immigrants have been part and parcel of U.S. society since the nineteenth century. They have as long a chronology as any other immigrant group. They are not social novelties, yet they are judged as aliens not warranting legal protections.

Secondly, Latinos draw a noticeable share of the phobias, biases, and stereotype allocations, which have been common to this society for generations. True, other immigrants in times past have been pejoratized, but the animus surrounding Latinos has persisted over generations.

Thirdly, there is a particular paradox to Latino immigrants. Indeed, factually demonstrable Latino immigrants are to date indispensable laborers in several sectors to the economy. This useful labor provision is understood to be useful to many, profitable to some. However, the work and the Latino individuals doing the work are disrespected. In fact, the disseminations of both convictions interact exponentially. Under these subjective constructions, can Latino immigrants claim their objective human rights and petitions for civil rights? Dr. Huerta answers, yes.

Dr. Huerta, an acknowledged scholar of immigration economics and policies, in these essays moves the debate on immigrants towards practical humanistic considerations. Indeed, there are inherent perceptual obstacles to common-sense public discussions. Ultimately, Dr. Huerta is an optimist, as we shall all be. Human issues can be resolved with humanistic solutions. Immigrants are not strangers; they are family.

Introduction

I wrote the majority of these essays while working on my dissertation at U.C. Berkeley's Department of City and Regional Planning, which I completed in the fall of 2011. When I first initiated my doctoral studies at Berkeley, I didn't plan on conducting research and writing about immigration issues in the U.S. Instead, my academic interests mainly focused on race, labor, social movements, Chicana/o studies, and the informal economy in urban settings. However, given the rise of xenophobia in this country, especially in the state of Arizona and the deep South, I felt compelled to respond to the lies and contradictions perpetuated by conservatives, Republicans, and Tea Party members against undocumented immigrants in this country. The draconian laws and racist attacks against undocumented immigrants have also manifested towards legalized immigrants and U.S.-born Latinas/os.

In this collection of essays—many of which appeared in numerous U.S. periodicals and online outlets—I reframe the portrayal of immigrants (and immigration policy) in the U.S. from a negative narrative to a positive one; from a simplistic argument to a nuanced understanding of human behavior; from an inhumane portrait of so-called "illegal immigrants" to a humane portrayal of honest, hard-working individuals struggling to survive and thrive in an often hostile environment.

Intended for a broad audience, the social commentary of these essays relies on many sources, including academic journals, newspaper articles, opinion editorials, news from national media outlets, and speeches by elected officials. I have also relied on my many years of civic engagement experience with immigrant communities and my own family history.

In short, I wrote these essays to challenge the preconceived and pejorative views that many Americans possess towards immigrants. Also, by exposing the lies and contradictions of those who peddle fear, blame, and displaced anger against vulnerable populations for personal or political benefit, I advocate vigorously for the humane treatment of *los de abajo* (those on the bottom) in this country.

Call for Humane Immigration Reform

The time has arrived for President Obama and Congress to take immediate action on comprehensive, humane immigration reform.

By immigration reform, I am not talking about militarizing our borders, empowering employers to behave as immigration enforcement officials, and imposing fines and back taxes on aspiring citizens. Instead, I am talking about allowing labor to cross our borders as transnational capital does, preventing employers from exploiting immigrant laborers, and lowering application costs for future citizens.

Too often, when Democratic and Republican leaders speak about comprehensive immigration reform, their message mainly centers on enforcement-dominated policies. For instance, while Obama spoke eloquently about immigrants in his second inaugural address, his administration has deported more immigrants than that of his predecessor, President Bush, during the same time period.

As the Obama administration continues to separate hard-working immigrants from their families and friends, I find it hard to believe the president when he says, "Our journey is not complete until we find a better way to welcome the striving, hopeful immigrants who still see America as a land of opportunity." I don't find the deportation of more than 1.6 million undocumented immigrants during Obama's first term in office as "welcoming."

Moreover, given that Republican leaders remain hostile and pay only lip service to Latinos and immigrants in this country, it's incumbent on Obama and Democratic leaders to invest the necessary political capital for the benefit of the estimated 11 million undocumented immigrants in this country. Instead of dehumanizing and blaming recent immigrants for America's financial woes, like the GOP does, Obama and Democratic leaders should demand that Latino immigrants be treated with dignity, respect, and tolerance.

More specifically, Democratic leaders should educate and convince the public about the pivotal role undocumented immigrants play in America's social and economic prosperity, highlighting key characteristics like their willingness to sacrifice themselves for their families, a strong work ethic, and an entrepreneurial bent. In developing a humane immigration reform policy, both Democrats and Republicans should learn from past immigrant policies with progressive elements. This includes the Immigration and Nationality Act of 1965, where immigrants from Latin America, Asia, and Africa benefited from family reunification components of the law. This also includes the Immigration Reform and Control Act of 1986, where almost 3 million immigrants qualified for amnesty. Republican leaders should learn from their iconic figure, President Reagan, who signed this legislation into law.

Instead of doing what's right in both moral and economic terms by proposing another amnesty plan, a recent bipartisan group of senators, also known as the Senate "Gang of Eight," introduced a regressive, comprehensive immigration reform proposal. It includes a so-called pathway to citizenship for qualified undocumented immigrants.

But it mainly focuses on punitive measures, such as a "secured border" prerequisite before granting citizenship, imposing fines and back taxes, deputizing employers to become more effective immigration enforcement officials, and creating an exploitable labor pool of guest workers, like the Bracero Program of the mid-20th century—a program that my father, Salomón Huerta Sr., participated in under inhumane working conditions.

In short, there's only one humane and simple plan for the estimated 11 million undocumented immigrants in this country: amnesty. Let's get over the hostility to the term, and welcome the people who have been working in the shadows.

Amnesty for Immigrants
(co-written with ANTONIA MONTES)

Before the end of the year, presidents often consider grants of pardon and amnesty. This year, 2012, President Obama should grant amnesty to the 11 million undocumented immigrants in America, excluding those guilty of heinous crimes like murder, rape, armed robbery, and child abuse.

Undocumented immigrants work hard, make great sacrifices, save their earnings, and rely primarily on themselves and their personal networks to survive in this country. They take jobs commonly discarded by average Americans due to low pay and low social status. From washing dishes to parking cars, from cleaning toilets to changing diapers (both for children and some elderly), from picking tomatoes to mowing lawns, immigrants toil daily in these so-called dirty jobs.

Yet Republican leaders, conservative activists, and right-wing talk-show hosts assail immigrants for allegedly taking American jobs and burdening our social welfare programs. But undocumented immigrants don't qualify for many state and federally funded safety-net programs, thanks to former President Bill Clinton's Welfare Reform Act of 1996 and other measures.

Also, while many undocumented immigrants incur payroll deductions and pay into the Social Security system, they aren't able to receive economic or medical benefits once they reach retirement age, such as Social Security or Medicare.

Essentially, these hard-working individuals put more into the system than they receive or consume—the exact opposite of their "free rider" depiction that conservatives so often use.

Moreover, by working for low wages (and, oftentimes, receiving below the federal minimum wage), immigrants generate labor cost savings for employers, who then sell their goods and services at lower prices to American consumers. For instance, how much would a house salad cost at a local restaurant if employers hired non-immigrant laborers to pick, package, deliver, prepare, and serve the lettuce and everything else that goes with it?

While it's easy for Republicans and their supporters to blame Latino immigrants for America's economic crises, it's hard for them to live without this important work force and the services that immigrants provide on a daily basis to American consumers. It's almost impossible for the average American to go a day without experiencing the benefit of immigrant labor at the local dry cleaner, grocery market, restaurant, car wash, office building, or hotel.

Instead of recognizing immigrants for their hard work by passing legislation that allows for these immigrants and their families to fix their legal status via amnesty, Republican leaders continue to balk at any just and humane reform that would offer a pathway to citizenship. Given the obstinacy of the Republicans, President Obama should take matters into his own hands and solve this problem once and for all. He should issue a blanket amnesty to all undocumented immigrants who have not committed violent crimes. It would be in keeping with this season of charity, and it would let 11 million hard-working people come out into the light of day.

Note: Antonia Montes is an educator and long-time advocate for the humane treatment of immigrants in the U.S.

Latino Immigrants and the 2012 Elections

President Barack Obama owes Latinos big-time for his 2012 re-election victory. According to the polling group Latino Decisions, Obama received an overwhelming 75 percent of the Latino vote. Representing 10 percent of the electorate, Latinos played a pivotal role in Obama's victory over former Governor Mitt Romney, particularly in key swing states such as Nevada, Florida, New Mexico, Virginia, and Colorado.

Now that the presidential election has concluded and national discussions of comprehensive immigration reform have become a priority for Republicans and Democrats, especially given the importance of the Latino vote in future elections, it's imperative for both parties to incorporate a pathway to citizenship as a central theme of any proposed legislation. If "comprehensive immigration reform" only means additional enforcement measures, such as more funding for high-tech border fences, enforcement officials, and work-site deportations, then we might as well tolerate the status quo.

While Obama enjoyed the majority of Latino votes, as well as those of Asian Americans, African Americans, gays, unmarried women, and young people, let's not forget that the president failed to deliver for Latinos during most of his first term in the area of immigration—an important issue to many Latinos (and Asians). Instead of supporting policies in defense of this growing voting and demographic group, in his first term, Obama has deported more undocumented immigrants compared to his predecessor, George W. Bush, during the same time frame.

For instance, according to *The Washington Post*, as of July, 2012, Obama's administration deported over 1.4 million undocumented immigrants.

In addition to deporting undocumented immigrants and separating families at a faster rate than Bush, Obama also failed to pass comprehensive immigration reform—an early promise he never kept—even when Democrats dominated both the Senate and House of Representatives for a short period. Also, unlike other important issues, such as health care and gay rights, Obama invested little or no political capital to pass the DREAM Act—the bill aimed at providing eligible young immigrants with a pathway to citizenship.

Moreover, Obama appears satisfied with two draconian, federal policies targeting mostly undocumented Latino immigrants: E-Verify and 287(g). While E-Verify—a voluntary federal program—allows for employers to verify the legal status of their employees utilizing hiring documents (the I-9 form) and government records, 287(g)—also a voluntary federal program—allows for state and local police authorities to operate as surrogates of the U.S. Immigration and Customs Enforcement (I.C.E.) officers by documenting and turning over suspected undocumented immigrants to federal authorities for possible deportation proceedings. While praised by many national leaders, political pundits, and elected officials—both Republicans and Democrats—these flawed programs instill a deep sense of fear and anxiety among the estimated 11 million undocumented immigrants in this country.

But instead of attacking Obama on these harsh and punitive measures, thereby eroding his support among Latinos, Romney and the Republican Party not only doubled down on these mostly enforcement policies, but went the extra mile to further target and vilify Latino immigrants at the local, state, and federal levels. While Romney praised Arizona's anti-immigrant law, SB 1070, requiring undocumented immigrants to carry with them federal registration papers, as a model for the entire country to follow, he also made his (in)famous remark about undocumented immigrants and "self-deportation" as part of his grand immigration plan.

Taking advantage of Romney's and the GOP's gross missteps on immigration and Latino communities, Obama smartly introduced an executive order to provide short-term relief to eligible undocumented youth against deportation proceedings. Referred to as "deferred action," eligible youth who apply will be granted legal protection to reside in the U.S. for a short period and allowed to work without a pathway to citizenship. While Obama clearly pandered to Latino voters for this much needed relief prior to election day, this program also has negative aspects for the young applicants, since the government will now have a huge database of their personal information, making them more vulnerable in the near future due to unforeseen consequences such as mass deportations.

Instead of making life more difficult for those who take care of our children, clean our homes (like my late mother did), wash our cars, and mow our front lawns, we, as a nation, should respect and treat the millions of immigrants who work and live in America's shadows as human beings. Thus, we should not punish them like common criminals, but reward them for their hard work ethic, daily sacrifices, and contributions to America's prosperity with a simple and humane plan: amnesty.

Echo Park, Los Angeles, CA, 1998

I Ain't No Anchor Baby

I'm the son of Mexican immigrants, but I ain't no anchor baby.

My late father, Salomón Chavez Huerta, Sr., first migrated to the United States during the 1950s via the Bracero Program, in which more than 4.6 million rural Mexicans performed desperately needed agricultural work in this country. He worked long hours, six days a week, for little pay, and under terrible conditions. Later, as a legal permanent resident, he performed factory work for decades at sub-minimum wage.

Meanwhile, my late mother, Carmen Mejia Huerta, originally came to this country during the 1960s, securing employment as a house cleaner for mostly white, middle-class families. Lacking formal education, like my father, she labored as a domestic worker for more than 40 years. This did not stop her, however, as a naturalized U.S. citizen, from seeking more clients in her twilight years.

Currently, Republican leaders, like Senate Minority Leader Mitch McConnell, R-KY, and Sen. Lindsey Graham, R-SC, are making a big fuss about the U.S.-born children of undocumented immigrants. They're calling for a change in the 14th Amendment of the Constitution, which stipulates that all persons born in the United States are citizens. According to Graham, undocumented immigrants come to this country simply to "drop a child," or what he pejoratively refers to as "drop and leave."

Republicans don't practice what they preach. While they endlessly talk about "family values" and the sanctity of the unborn child, when it comes to Latino immigrants, they defame the family unit and attack brown children.

Republican leaders are consciously instilling fear in the American public by scapegoating Latinos (both documented and undocumented) in this country. Let's not forget that the controversial Arizona law (SB 1070), now held up in court, required police to stop anyone they suspected was here illegally—and that could mean all brown-skinned people.

Responding to the Republican anti-immigrant agenda, Senate Majority Leader Harry Reid, D-NV, properly questioned how any person of Latino heritage could be a Republican. Reid should be applauded for calling out Latino Republicans for belonging to a political party that is hostile to them.

Instead of dealing with appalling unemployment figures, high home foreclosure rates, and lack of credit for small businesses, Republicans are targeting the most vulnerable population in this country: undocumented immigrants. By doing so, they are no different from schoolyard bullies.

Didn't they learn basic manners, such as treating others with respect and dignity? I certainly learned those lessons from my parents.

My parents taught my siblings and me to be good and generous to others. They also encouraged us to pursue higher education so that we don't experience the same hardships they faced both in Mexico and this country. My late parents came to this country to seek work and a better life for themselves and their family.

They sacrificed themselves—toiling in back-breaking, low-wage, dead-end jobs—so their children could pursue better opportunities not available in their homeland.

Instead of praising them for their sacrifice and hard work, Republicans continue to bash and tarnish the memory of my late parents and the millions of others like them in this country. This is shameful.

The Privileged Need to Show Consideration for the Poor

The poor get no respect in this country. As someone who experienced abject poverty in America's barrios, I know a thing or two about being disrespected due to my family's reliance on government aid for a temporary period. When I was growing up, we received welfare, food stamps, Medicaid, and public housing. Although my Mexican immigrant parents never committed any crimes, I felt a deep sense of shame, thanks to the slurs of many elected officials, public figures, and media outlets.

Recently, Republicans have taken a leadership role in bashing the poor. GOP presidential contender Mitt Romney said that he doesn't care too much for them. Newt Gingrich, another presidential aspirant, wants to do away with child labor laws, since inner-city kids "ought to learn how to go to work." Gingrich also has referred to President Obama, on more than one occasion, as the "food stamp president." Democratic leaders have failed to respond sufficiently by defending food stamps and other important safety-net programs for those in need, especially during the terrible economic times we've been in.

It's no secret why the poor receive little attention from both Republicans and Democrats during election seasons. Poor people lack the financial resources to make political contributions to political candidates and, now, the all-powerful Super PACs.

Disrespecting the poor is not new in America. Prior to the Great Depression, many politicians and national leaders also treated the poor with disdain. In the early 1900s, the powerful and rich commonly used words like "lazy" and "freeloaders" to describe the poor, placing the full burden of their bleak plight solely on their shoulders.

It wasn't until the market crashed in 1929 and the middle class and some members of the upper class directly suffered that many Americans came to the harsh realization that structural factors affect individual behavior and outcomes. If there's a silver lining in this country's economic calamities, it is that many Americans understand that financial markets periodically create uncertainty for the majority, while a privileged minority remains insulated.

Republican presidential candidates can rail all they want against food stamps, but for millions of Americans who, due to no fault of their own, have had to rely on them to feed themselves and their families, the simple reality is this: the private sector left them stranded; only government assistance has kept them fed.

Making food stamps a campaign issue is a loser for Republicans. Too many Americans now recognize how vital the program is.

El Bordo, Tijuana, Mexico, 1989

Romney's Anti-immigration Will Haunt Him in 2012 Presidential Election

Mitt Romney may well be on his way to the Republican nomination, but he'll have a hard time getting further than that because of his position on immigration. Romney's hostile stance against even immigrant children who arrived here when they were very young does not sit well with Latinos, to say the least.

Like all voting groups, Latino registered voters represent a heterogeneous group of individuals with diverse political viewpoints and backgrounds, from liberal to moderate to conservative. This includes Chicanos from East Los Angeles, Puerto Ricans from the Bronx, and Cubans from "Little Havana" in Miami.

However, as a voting bloc, Latino voters tend to support the rights of undocumented immigrants and vote Democrat at a higher rate compared to all registered voters. For instance, according to a recent poll from the Pew Hispanic Center, while 42 percent of all Latino registered voters favor a pathway to citizenship for the 11 million undocumented immigrants in this country, only 24 percent of all registered voters support this position. Also, in a hypothetical matchup between President Obama and Romney for the 2012 election, an overwhelming 68 percent of all Latino voters favor Obama, while only 23 percent support Romney.

Obama gave Romney an opening with Latinos, as 59 percent of Latinos disapprove of Obama's inhumane deportation policy of breaking up families. But Romney didn't take it. Instead, he has tacked to the right on the immigration issue. He has denounced Texas Governor Rick Perry for approving in-state tuition for immigrant students, claiming this represents a magnet for illegal immigration. He recently vowed to veto the DREAM Act, which would enable children of undocumented immigrants to become citizens if they go to college or serve in the military, and he opposes any amnesty for undocumented immigrants, despite their daily contributions to this country.

All undocumented immigrants, Romney says, should return to their country of birth and then get in the back of the line if they want to re-enter the United States legally. These views do not endear Romney to Latinos, who represent a growing—and perhaps pivotal—voter bloc. Romney's anti-immigrant stance may be helping him win the Republican nomination but is spoiling his chance to win the White House. He may have plenty of time on his hands, after November, to ponder that irony.

Alabama's Racist Immigration Law:
From Jim Crow to Juan Crow

When it comes to scapegoating immigrants for America's woes, the Deep South takes the cake. From slavery to Jim Crow—legalized, racial segregation—to the recent wave of anti-immigration rhetoric and policies, the South has taken the lead, once again, in passing the harshest, most racist laws against *los de abajo* / those on the bottom.

Not wanting to be outdone by other xenophobic states, such as Arizona, Utah, Indiana, and Georgia, Alabama Governor Robert Bentley signed HB 56 into law on June 6, 2011. This harsh law targets undocumented immigrants in numerous areas, such as public benefits, employment, housing, public education, and law enforcement. It also promotes racial profiling against all Latinos, with or without legal status in this country, since the law requires that police officers inquire into the citizenship status of all individuals under the guise of "reasonable suspicion." It doesn't take a scientific study to predict that those most likely to be targeted will be brown-skinned individuals. In addition to making police officers take on the role of immigration agents or *la migra*, as Mexican immigrants "fondly" refer to them, HB 56 also transforms teachers and school officials into feared immigration agents by requiring them to check the legal status of all K-12 children. If instilling fear into innocent, Spanish-speaking children isn't cruel and unusual punishment, I don't know what is.

There are other racist elements to this law. For instance, a U.S. citizen can be arrested for "harboring" an undocumented immigrant by simply having him or her over for a family celebration. Landlords will also be legally liable for renting to someone who lacks legal status in this country, prompting them to avoid renting to anyone named Jose, Jesus, or Maria. In addition, single mothers or the elderly can run afoul of the law by simply hiring a day laborer from the street corner or a home-improvement center like Home Depot for moving heavy furniture or clearing dangerous brush from the front yard that may cause fires.

For those of us who believe in equality and social justice for all individuals, especially the most vulnerable among us, we need to re-frame the issue of immigration as a matter of human rights. If we limit the national debate on immigration reform, for instance, to a false dichotomy between "law-abiding citizens" and "law-breaking immigrants," then those who advocate for fear and hate win.

The anti-immigration leaders in this country, especially the Republican leaders who are spearheading these xenophobic efforts, constantly preach about freedom, liberty, and justice for all. They especially warn us about government intrusion into our lives. Don't these principles also apply to Latinos, who will also be the victims of big government in the form of immigration laws that promote racial profiling?

While I can understand that many Americans face uncertain and fearful times in this Great Recession, however, I find it unacceptable for them to constantly blame undocumented immigrants for America's economic downfall. Like the previous millions of Europeans who abandoned their homelands due to religious persecution, war, and economic upheaval, so, too, do these newcomers from Latin America and beyond arrive in this country to seek a better life for themselves and their families.

It's clear that Republican leaders know that these cruel state laws, such as the cases of Arizona's SB 1070 and Alabama's HB 56, will be contested in the courts on constitutional grounds. They are well aware that the federal government—not the states—has jurisdiction over immigration law. Why, then, do they pursue this state-by-state, anti-immigration law strategy? Simply put, Republican leaders are counting that these state laws will inevitably go to the conservative-dominated Supreme Court, with the hopes of legalizing xenophobia in this country.

In the end, if the Republican leaders inevitably prevail at the Supreme Court, it will not be the first time the highest court of the land ruled in favor of legalized racism, as we can clearly see in the cases of slavery and the Jim Crow era, when racial segregation prevailed for many years throughout American neighborhoods, public schools, public places, transportation, private business, government programs, and the military.

If the majority of Americans don't act now and demand that their elected officials seek a humane immigration policy throughout the country, we should not be surprised if Juan Crow soon replaces the odious Jim Crow.

Echo Park, Los Angeles, CA, 1998

Republicans Need to Stop Blaming Immigrants

The scapegoating of immigrants must stop. Whether it's Sen. John McCain, R-AZ, blaming the wildfires in the southwest on immigrants coming across the border, or it's the state of Alabama passing the harshest anti-immigrant law in the country, it's clear that brown-skinned immigrants have become the targets of the day. We've moved from the era of Jim Crow—with legalized, racial segregation against blacks—to the era of what I call Juan Crow, with legalized, racial discrimination against Latinos.

McCain said there was "substantial evidence that some of these fires have been caused by people who have crossed our border illegally." But he didn't provide that evidence, and police have not arrested anyone yet, so his comment was reckless and irresponsible. McCain's remark is in keeping with the xenophobic legislation that has become law in such states as Arizona, Georgia, Indiana, and Utah, and now Alabama has topped them all after Gov. Robert Bentley signed HB 56 into law on June 9, 2011. That law invites racial profiling of Latinos, both permanent residents and citizens, since the law requires that police officers inquire into the citizenship status of an individual (most likely brown-skinned) if the officers have "reasonable suspicion" that the person is not here legally. In addition to making police officers immigration agents, HB 56 also transforms teachers into immigration agents by requiring them to check the citizenship status of all K-12 children.

Landlords also will be conscripted as immigration agents, since the law makes them legally liable for renting to someone without proper citizenship documentation.

Under the new Alabama law, a U.S. citizen can be arrested for "harboring" an undocumented immigrant by simply having someone without legal status in his or her home for a family gathering. In addition, an elderly person can easily run afoul of the law by hiring a day laborer on the corner to help with moving furniture or performing yard work, since the law prohibits any employment of undocumented immigrants in the state.

This law, like similar ones in other states, runs counter to the Christian principles of "love thy neighbor" and "treat others as you wish to be treated." While it's understandable that most Americans are feeling frustrated and frightened in this Great Recession, it's not acceptable for many of them to scapegoat the most vulnerable in this country: undocumented immigrants. These individuals come to this country to work hard and make an honest living for themselves and families, like the previous millions of Europeans who settled in this country during time of war and economic upheaval in their own homelands. Just as the era of Jim Crow came to be known as a moral failing on the part of those who constructed it and benefited from it, so, too, will this era of Juan Crow.

Real Immigration Reform Needed, Not Just Words

President Obama's recent immigrant speech in El Paso, Texas, amounted to "much ado about nothing" for Latinos. Instead of sympathetic words for immigrants in a re-election, campaign-style format, we need for Obama to make immigration reform a top priority in lieu of pandering to a growing Latino electorate.

Presidents, throughout U.S. history, employ catchy phrases to identify their administrations' policy priorities. We have, for example, President Lyndon B. Johnson's "War on Poverty," President Ronald Reagan's "War on Drugs," and—how can we forget?—President George W. Bush's "War on Terror." In this tradition, we need for President Obama to wage the "War on Xenophobia" campaign as a key part of his presidency.

Just like his predecessors, Obama's "War on Xenophobia" campaign, or humane immigration reform, should include concrete plans of action, lobbying efforts with Congress, executive orders, legislative bills, allocated funding, Blue Ribbon Commissions, and the necessary political capital investment to ensure victory. Obama should push for a humane immigration reform policy to counter the Republican's state-by-state xenophobia strategy. In doing so, Obama needs to be consistent.

While hectoring Republicans on the plight of undocumented immigrants and asking the GOP to acknowledge those who come to this country to "earn a living and provide for their families," Obama has outpaced Bush in terms of actual deportations. This not only includes immigrants with major and minor criminal records, including those wrongfully convicted, but also honest, hard-working individuals who obey the laws, purchase goods, and contribute more to the economy than they receive in return.

Where's the humanity that Obama talks about when a U.S.-born child comes home only to learn that her Mexican immigrant mother was deported? Where's the justice that Obama talks about when 11 million undocumented workers toil in low-paying jobs that most Americans reject yet benefit from in the form of cheap goods and services?

Because Latinos represent more than 50 million individuals of the total U.S. population, neither Obama nor the next Republican presidential candidate can afford to take this ethnic group for granted, especially since Latinos generally favor a humane immigration policy over the existing, unjust, and broken system.

Take, for example, the DREAM Act—a bill aimed at helping qualified undocumented students and those who serve in the military with a pathway towards citizenship. While Obama supports this bill, he hasn't done enough to get the Republican votes.

If Obama truly supports Latinos in general and immigrants in particular, why didn't he push for reform late last year in Congress before the Republicans killed the DREAM Act? Why didn't Obama play hardball with the Republicans, demanding the GOP's support for the bill, when they wanted to extend the Bush taxes for the rich?

Given that the Republicans prioritized the tax cuts for the rich over any other policy issue, including high unemployment rates and rising housing foreclosures, Obama had the perfect opportunity to get this bill passed. Instead, it died in Congress, like the dreams of countless immigrant students and those serving in the military.

If Obama isn't willing to risk his political capital, especially now with favorable poll numbers after the killing of Osama bin Laden, what makes the more than 50 million Latinos in this country think that Obama will pass a humane immigration reform bill anytime soon?

Anapara, TX, 2003

Defeat of Dream Act Will Haunt Republicans

Republicans managed to defeat the DREAM Act, but it's a victory that will haunt them. The DREAM Act—the Development, Relief and Education for Alien Minors Act—died in the Senate on Dec. 18, just five votes away from the 60 needed to advance. The Republican Party once again demonstrated its disdain toward one of the most marginalized and vulnerable groups in this country: undocumented immigrants.

Let's not forget the Democrats who voted against it. This group included Sens. Max Baucus of Montana, Kay Hagan of North Carolina, Ben Nelson of Nebraska, Mark Pryor of Arkansas, and Jon Tester of Montana. If passed in Congress and signed into law by President Obama, the DREAM Act would have provided a pathway to citizenship to many undocumented individuals, demonstrating a strong commitment toward higher education or service in the military.

I had several reservations about this bill, but not the same ones that the senators voting "no" had. I didn't like the word "Alien" in the title; no human being is an alien. I didn't like the fact that it would have induced young brown people to risk their lives in unjust wars like the one President Bush waged in Iraq, and I didn't like the fact that it gave special treatment to those who attend college. An immigrant kid who doesn't go to college still contributes to our society, after all.

Apart from my objections, this bill should have passed. It would have given hope and opportunity to immigrant children who came to this country at least five years ago—often as youngsters. At the end of the day, while this is a short-term loss for Latinos in this country, in the long term the Republicans and those conservative Democrats will pay a big price at the ballot box.

The browning of America is a reality that an aging white population needs to come to terms with. As the largest racial minority group in the country with a higher birth rate than the national average, Latinos will inevitably represent a majority in many key states. Latinos are rising up and demanding to be treated as human beings—with or without legal status. We want our children to have an equal shot at the American dream, and not experience an American nightmare.

From Teen Day Laborer to Urban Planning Scholar

In light of the rampant xenophobia in this country, I reflect on the lessons that I learned as a teen day laborer many years ago. Working alongside Latino immigrant men during a hot summer in Malibu, I learned first-hand the trials and tribulations of manual labor. This grueling experience became the impetus for my academic trajectory, scholarship, and lifelong commitment to social justice. While most of my childhood friends played basketball at East L.A.'s Ramona Gardens housing project, my brother Salomón Huerta, Jr.—now an acclaimed L.A.-based artist—and I performed landscaping duties as day laborers for the wealthy in the seaside city.

When it came to manual labor, as a 13-year-old I represented the typical U.S.-born kid who avoided physical work like the plague. I can still hear the voice of my late mother, Carmen Mejia Huerta, telling me to clean my room and make my bed. Miraculously, she kept our rooms tidy while toiling as a house cleaner on the Westside, a job she performed for over 40 years. Despite the fact that I excelled in school, especially in mathematics, my mother—a Mexican immigrant—always encouraged my siblings and me to do well in school. Like most immigrant parents, she implored us to maximize our educational opportunities to avoid the pitfalls of immigrant jobs associated with meager wages, low status, and dismal upward mobility options.

Given that she couldn't help me with my algebra, my mother did what any rational woman in her situation would do: she told my late father, Salomón Chavez Huerta, Sr., to take my brother and me to work as day laborers. To borrow from President Obama's lexicon, she created a "teachable moment" for us. My father originally came to this country as an agricultural guest worker under the Bracero Program during the 1950s. For him, working as a day laborer represented a walk in the park. For my brother and me, however, it was a nightmare.

First, we had to wake up at 5 a.m. Then we took a two-hour bus from the Eastside to the Westside. Thereafter, we joined other day laborers to compete for scarce resources. Never in my life had I witnessed a group of grown men vying for the attention of wealthy whites in their BMWs and Mercedes Benzes; the drivers sought men to do tasks from digging ditches and clearing brush to painting homes and loading trucks.

I was initially embarrassed to see my father—a proud Mexican immigrant—running toward the luxury cars, trying to convince the driver to select him and his two young sons. I always wondered how this impacted his manhood and self-esteem. This is an entirely different world from that of privileged children, who see their parents go off to work as doctors, lawyers, and CEOs.

Once my father secured a landscaping job for us, the day only worsened for me. Like most children of immigrants, I was translating for my father with the employer regarding our measly wages and job duties. I felt like a prisoner negotiating with the warden for my undesirable work assignment. It was only 8 a.m., and I found myself with the laborious task of pulling weeds all day. Just like when I attended church, I checked my watch every second, wondering when the work would end. My back, knees, and arms ached after hours of pulling weeds from an enormous and idyllic backyard.

"OK," my father said in Spanish. "It's time." Thinking the job ended, I rejoiced. I quickly realized that it was only lunchtime with another four hours to go. Not saying a word, I had my first epiphany: I have no other option but to attend U.C.L.A.

Now that my 11-year-old son has entered his final year of elementary school, my wife, Antonia, and I regularly discuss which prestigious university he will attend. Unlike my wife and I—who grew up with parents from rural Mexico without formal educations—our son has two parents with advanced degrees from the best universities in the world: U.C.L.A. and U.C. Berkeley. Apart from having a mother as an educator at the primary and university levels, he will very soon have a father with a Ph.D., working as a professor at a major university.

While we regularly take our son to educational trips and museums—including math clubs, chess tournaments, soccer lessons, and community service activities—that will foster his success in school and life, I can't wait until he turns 13 so that he, too, can learn first-hand from the honest, hard-working men who seek work every morning on the corners of America's cities and suburbs. These Latino immigrant men are not the so-called villains whom Republican leaders scapegoat for America's ills. They are decent human beings who deserve to be treated with respect and dignity.

In short, day laborers, like Latina domestic workers, should be treated as honorable individuals for their hard work and sacrifice in order to provide for their families. From my personal and scholarly perspective, they are true heroes.

East L.A., CA, 2003

Respect for the People Who Grow Your Garden

As Congress and the White House quibble over the best policies and programs to revive the sluggish economy—from tax relief to public infrastructure projects to small business aid—who's advocating for the countless self-employed individuals in this country? This includes a significant number of individuals who engage in a variety of economic activities as independent contractors, such as plumbers, mechanics, electricians, after-school tutors, fishermen, tax preparers, and those who toil in the domestic household service economy.

The domestic household economy encompasses house cleaners, paid gardeners and, very often, day laborers. This mostly Latino immigrant work force in California and beyond has taken over the traditional household duties and responsibilities that many Americans assumed prior to WWII, where women regularly stayed home to care for the children and clean the home, while men worked outdoors to "master" the front lawn—an American obsession of the archetypal suburban home.

While my late mother, Carmen Mejia Huerta, worked as a house cleaner for more than 40 years in this country, my dissertation research project at U.C. Berkeley focuses on paid Latino gardeners and their social networks in Los Angeles' unregulated economy.

My initial scholarly interest to better understand this group goes back to my days as a community activist when I and fellow activists Adrian Alvarez, Antonia Montes, and others originally helped organize this informal work-force in response to the City of Los Angeles' leaf-blower ban.

We first learned about the city's plans by a veteran paid gardener, Jaime Aleman, who emerged as an organic leader in this social justice battle. Led by the late council member Marvin Braude, in May 14, 1996, the Los Angeles City Council voted 9 to 4 to ban leaf blowers within a residential area. The heavy penalties for a paid gardener caught using this work device included a misdemeanor charge, $1,000 fine, and up to six months in jail. In response, the Latino gardeners founded the Association of Latin American Gardeners of Los Angeles and initiated one of the most dynamic social justice movements since the "Justice for Janitors" campaign of the early 1990s and United Farm Workers' cause of the 1960s.

Following numerous protests, marches, press conferences, candlelight vigils, and a week-long hunger strike, the Latino gardeners eventually prevailed, forcing the city to dramatically amend this law.

While the affluent Westsiders, who favored the ban, framed this issue as a public nuisance, focusing on issues of noise and pollution, the Latino gardeners successfully re-framed the issue as the "haves against the have-nots." In the end, the Latino gardeners prevailed in the court of public opinion.

Going beyond the contentious leaf-blower issue, I've spent the last several years conducting archival and field research on the history of paid gardening in this country and how it currently operates. Like an anthropologist who lives with villagers in Guatemala, I've gained the trust of these individuals and spent many hours with them.

They allowed me to enter their universe. By doing so, I've developed a more comprehensive understanding of how this informal market is organized, how it works, and the roles of the various individuals involved.

Countering the stereotypical portrayals of paid gardeners in Hollywood, television, and the mainstream media, where these individuals represent so-called "ignorant workers" with little to contribute, over the years I've found these people to be highly intelligent, productive members of society. Despite lacking human capital (higher education and special training) and financial capital, many of these Latino immigrant men are sophisticated individuals who own and operate their own small businesses. They engage, for example, in complex entrepreneurial transactions on a regular basis, such as expanding business operations, developing client routes, billing and receiving, trading, and selling goods or services with other small businesses.

In the case of Jaime Aleman, a naturalized citizen from Zacatecas, Mexico, who has owned and operated a successful gardening business for the past two decades, we can see how these people have created successful enterprises outside the formal economy. Given the lack of educational opportunities in his rural hometown, Aleman joined his father and brothers in the agricultural fields at the tender age of 10 years old. Once immigrating to the U.S., he wasted no time joining the work force to one day become self-employed.

As an owner of a small gardening enterprise, Aleman is a productive member of society and positive role model due to his perseverance in life, strong work ethic, and entrepreneurial spirit. Like the Japanese immigrant gardeners of the last century, paid gardeners, like Aleman and his colleagues, contribute daily towards making our communities greener, cleaner, safer, and more beautiful.

Thus, it's time for the government to make an investment in this green work force, especially during this great recession. Equally important, it's time for the public to appreciate Latino gardeners as honest, hard-working people who make positive contributions to America's cities and suburbs.

Anapara, TX, 2003

Forty Years Later, Grape Boycott Still Huge Accomplishment

Forty years ago, workers in the United States won a great victory. On July 29, 1970, the United Farm Workers of America (U.F.W.) ended its successful grape boycott when the growers agreed to sign the first contract with the union. It seemed like an improbable outcome, as the battle pitted a mostly Mexican as well as Filipino immigrant work force against powerful agricultural growers in California. Led by the late Cesar Chavez and tireless Dolores Huerta, the U.F.W. was founded in the early 1960s in response to the inhumane working conditions for farm workers in California and other states, such as Arizona, Texas, Florida, and Washington state.

While many American workers during this period enjoyed the right to organize, 40-hour weeks, minimum wage, and relatively safe working conditions, farm workers lacked these basic rights and protections. In an effort to seek justice, dignity, and respect in the rural fields of America, U.F.W. leaders, its members, and sympathizers organized and joined picket lines and marches, signed petitions, supported labor laws, lobbied elected officials, distributed educational flyers, produced documentaries, penned songs, performed plays, held teach-ins, and generally supported the nationwide boycott.

The charismatic Chavez—who graced the cover of *Time* magazine on July 4, 1969—engaged in numerous and lengthy hunger strikes to draw attention to the cause.

As was the case with the civil-rights movement, many U.F.W. activists were beaten up, and a few were killed for the simple act of supporting the right of farm workers to organize a union and negotiate for fair labor contracts. But the rightness of their cause prevailed. So inspirational was it that Barack Obama, when he was a candidate for president, adopted the group's slogan: "*Sí, Se Puede*" ("Yes, We Can").

Now, 40 years later, farm workers continue to toil under harsh working conditions. To draw attention to this, the U.F.W. has launched an innovative campaign called "Take Our Jobs," which encourages unemployed Americans to work in the agricultural fields to pick fruits and vegetables as a means to educating the public about the importance of immigrant labor issues and desperate need for humane labor reforms at the national level. As part of this campaign, U.F.W. President Arturo Rodriguez appeared on "The Colbert Report," the popular cable show, to shed light on the plight of "*los de abajo*" (those on the bottom).

The best way to honor this 40th anniversary of the U.F.W.'s landmark success would be to support humane labor law reform for farm workers and to strengthen the right to organize. *Sí, Se Puede*!

Arizona Gov. Jan Brewer Fears and Loathes Brown People

Not to be outdone by the late segregationist, Alabama Governor George Wallace, Arizona Gov. Jan Brewer will go down in the history books as an ardent xenophobe and racist. Brewer's hatred of immigrants and disregard for the civil rights of Latinos (both legal residents and citizens) have come to fruition in Arizona's recently passed laws aimed at criminalizing immigrants, racially profiling Latinos, and denying racial minorities the right to learn about their history.

I'm speaking, of course, of SB 1070, the unconstitutional law that requires police officers to demand legal documentation of individuals suspected of being undocumented immigrants under the premise of "reasonable suspicion," and HB 2281, the racist law that bans ethnic studies (optional courses, as a matter of fact) in public schools. Instead of chastising Brewer for her racist legislative actions, President Barack Obama recently invited her to the White House to discuss the controversial immigration law that the president referred to as "misguided." This is the same president who had a "Beer Summit" at the White House with a racist police officer, Sgt. James Crowley, shortly after he arrested Harvard Professor Henry Louis Gates, Jr.—a distinguished African American scholar—in his own home. This high-profile arrest can be traced to Gates' initial "inability" to verify proof of residence to Crowley even after Gates provided his Harvard faculty identification card.

As any parent should know, this is no way of rewarding bad behavior! Better yet, instead of meeting with Brewer in a one-to-one meeting usually afforded to world leaders, Obama should chastise the rogue governor and take direct action against Arizona's racist agenda. Obama can learn a thing or two from previous presidents. For instance, in 1963, then-President John F. Kennedy federalized the Alabama National Guard when Gov. Wallace attempted to prevent two African American students from attending the University of Alabama under a federal court order to desegregate public schools.

An ardent segregationist, Wallace, who operated under the political platform "segregation now, segregation tomorrow, segregation forever," eventually caved under pressure when confronted by the military might of the federal government. Taking this historical event as a "teachable moment," Obama needs to use all of executive powers, including unmatchable oratory skills, to immediately repeal both SB 1070 and HB 2281. While Obama and U.S. Attorney General Eric Holder contemplate legal action, individuals of Mexican descent in this desert state live in a constant state of fear, anxiety, and financial insecurity.

When she originally signed SB 1070 into law on April 23, 2010, Brewer assured the public that racial profiling would not be tolerated.

However, what does she—a white, privileged politician—know about racial profiling? I wonder if she, or any member of her family, has even been a victim of racial profiling? More specifically, has she ever been denied a taxicab in the city of New York or other major city because of the color of her skin? Has she ever been pulled over by a police officer for simply being in the "wrong neighborhood" or because she allegedly "matched the description" of someone suspected of committing a crime?

While Brewer and the supporters of this anti-immigrant law attempt to frame this policy measure as one of "crime" and "safety," especially with the law's official name, "Support Our Law Enforcement and Safe Neighborhoods Act," they have yet to produce any hard data correlating immigration with crime in the state. There is a word in the dictionary for making false accusations: slander. While much of the attention in the media has been given to this cruel immigration law, Brewer wasted no time in attacking the Latino community, once again, with the elimination of ethnic studies programs in public schools.

In an Orwellian maneuver, Brewer, the architect of this ban—Arizona's school chief Tom Horne—and other supporters argue that ethnic studies programs allegedly promote ethnic chauvinism, reverse racism against whites, and the overthrow of the U.S. government.

It is amazing how educational programs aimed at providing a more ethnically diverse interpretation of American life and history have now become eminent enemies of the state.

For instance, how is teaching a Latino high school student about the United Farm Workers (U.F.W.) and the fact that Cesar Chavez was born in Yuma, Arizona, suddenly un-American? How is teaching a young Latina student about Dolores Huerta, the co-founder of the U.F.W., now a criminal act? Does this mean that Latino and Asian students can't learn about the unconscionable Japanese American internment camps, where the state of Arizona hosted one, during the mid-20th century, since this falls under the purview of "ethnic studies" programs? The only logical conclusion here is an obvious attempt by those in power to erase the history of discrimination and social injustice committed against racial minorities in the state and beyond.

Finally, if we critically examine the motives behind these anti-Latino laws, it's clear that many people in Arizona and beyond fear and loathe the long-term consequence of Mexican immigration in particular and the demographic boom of Latinos in general, resulting in the browning of America.

El Paso, TX, 2001

Similarities Between Arizona Bill and BP Oil Spill

What does the State of Arizona have in common with BP, the British global energy corporation? Well, let me count the ways.

First, both have been spewing toxins into America's environment since late April of 2010. In the case of Arizona, Gov. Jan Brewer signed into law an unconstitutional and racist measure (SB 1070), criminalizing undocumented workers and legalizing racial profiling against Latinos. As for BP, this corporate mammoth, in the spirit of "drill baby drill," caused the largest oil-leak disaster since the infamous Exxon Valdez oil spill more than two decades ago.

Secondly, both have been grossly inaccurate regarding their data to rationalize their claims. The supporters of Arizona's immigration law argue that since undocumented workers account for the "rise of crime" in this state, the state government had no choice but to pass a law curtailing these so-called criminals. Yet recent reports show that crime has declined in the desert state, and the cheerleaders of this draconian law have yet to produce any legitimate data correlating immigrants with crime.

Thirdly, the actions of both the Arizona government and BP corporate leaders have caused more economic hardship for the residents of the already economically depressed regions.

In the case of Arizona, the growing national boycotts against this financially struggling state have resulted in the loss of revenue (both current and future) that will further damage the fragile economy already affected by the housing crises, credit crises, and overall current recession. As a former constitutional law professor and, now, the most powerful person in the world, President Obama should deliver a legal viewpoint and moral condemnation of a law that goes back to the dark days of Jim Crow of legalized racism. This immigration law not only violates federal law but also creates a new round of civil-rights violations against a particular racial group: Latinos.

As for BP, the Obama administration has also been too slow regarding the out-of-control oil leak. From the start, Obama should've been on the ground to put pressure on BP and should've taken full control to fix the leak since the London-based corporation doesn't appear to be capable of stopping it any time.

In short, in order to stop racist laws and disastrous oil leaks from occurring in this country, the federal government, in conjunction with the public, needs to take more proactive and aggressive measures to prevent state governments and corporate officials from spewing pollutants into our environment, with short- and long-term disastrous costs.

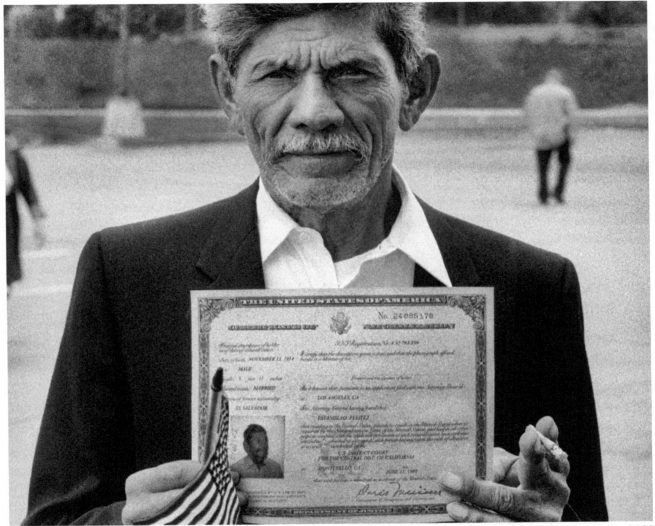

Receiving U.S. Citizenship, Los Angeles, CA, 2003

Immigration Bill Adds Little
to Comprehensive Reform

As the son of poor Mexican immigrants, I'm skeptical about comprehensive immigration reform aimed at helping undocumented workers in this xenophobic climate. While both Republicans and Democrats speak about America's dysfunctional immigration policies and the desperate need for immigration reform, the primary consensus between both political parties focuses on the need for tougher enforcement. The focus here is to criminalize undocumented immigrants, deporting them, and preventing future low-wage immigrants from entering this country.

Where's the humane discourse in this political debate? Are we not talking about human beings with ambitions and dreams to better themselves and their families? Are we not talking about vulnerable individuals who sacrifice so much with their bodies and labor power so that Americans can live more comfortable lives? Instead of having a civil conversation based on justice, dignity, and respect, too many elected officials and Americans talk about immigrants like extra-terrestrial invaders who come to this country to threaten the so-called American way of life.

This anti-immigrant hysteria usually escalates in times of economic and political crisis, when some Americans seek out scapegoats. During the Great Depression, the U.S. government engaged in a vicious campaign to deport Mexican immigrants.

In 1954, the anti-immigrant agenda reached a climax with "Operation Wetback," when the government deported hundreds of thousands of Mexican immigrants, including U.S. citizens of Mexican descent. While mass deportations of this scale remain part of America's dark past, anti-immigrant campaigns continue to the present. Throughout the country, we see federal, state, and local authorities, as in the case of Arizona's Sheriff Joe Arpaio, violate the human rights of immigrants on a routine basis.

Operating under the false assumption that undocumented immigrants represent law-breakers who should be treated like common criminals, elected officials and many Americans conveniently ignore one simple fact: America's dependency on low-wage immigrant workers. Like drug addicts, Americans are hooked on cheap immigrant labor from Mexico and beyond. Immigrants, for instance, play a major role in almost all aspects of America's economy. This includes agriculture, manufacturing, food processing, textiles, construction, retail, restaurants, electronics, tourism, and domestic household industries.

It's this contradiction that needs to be considered while Democrats and Republicans ponder comprehensive immigration reform. While it's easy to blame the supply side of this equation, elected officials also need to consider the demand side. In other words, immigrants are here because there's a demand for their labor, where both employers and consumers benefit in the forms of cheap labor and low-cost goods and services.

Immigrants are also active entrepreneurs. By starting ethnic businesses, immigrants hire workers and provide low-cost goods and services for local economies. This includes not only Koreans, Chinese, and Japanese immigrants, but also Salvadorans, Cubans, and Mexicans in major metropolitan areas like Los Angeles, the Bay Area, Miami, and New York.

It's a shame that Americans have taken the low road in a highly globalized economy, where markets have become more open, interconnected, and fluid. If the United States can have free-trade agreements with Canada and Mexico, such as N.A.F.T.A., along with other Latin American countries, why not take the same approach with labor?

Unfortunately, members of both parties continue to cling to creating a temporary guest-worker program, an archaic proposal that doesn't position our economy for the future. We don't need more programs aimed solely at benefiting American interests at the cost of the less fortunate. For instance, during the mid-20th century, the U.S.-supported guest-worker program, the Bracero Program, recruited more than 4 million Mexican immigrants—including my father, several uncles, and grandfather—to meet the major labor shortage in the agricultural sector.

Instead of being appreciated for their labor and efforts, these hard-working men faced racism, exploitation, and humiliation. Not only did they work long hours and live in overcrowded housing facilities, but they were also treated like livestock. For example, upon re-registering for the program in Mexico, these proud men were forced to strip naked without any privacy and sprayed with chemicals prior to entering the United States.

Now that the Democrats recently introduced a new immigration bill, spearheaded by Illinois Congressman Luis Gutierrez, we see the same language of heavy enforcement and a proposal for a temporary guest-worker program. The bill includes a potential pathway for citizenship for some of the 11 million undocumented individuals in this country, but even this is not guaranteed. As with the case of the health-care reform bill, there is a potential for mischief at the last moment. What guarantees do immigrants have that, at the last minute, a Blue Dog Democrat won't remove the most promising aspect of this latest immigration bill?

Thus, while the current immigration system may be dysfunctional, the odds of a more punitive immigration system remain high in the current environment. That will not change until more Americans make a break from their xenophobic roots.

A Green Immigration: Appreciating Paid Mexican Gardeners

The environmentalist movement in this country is no longer confined to a small group of so-called tree huggers and back-to-nature utopians. From Washington, D.C., to Los Angeles, the greening of the urban landscape has become trendy. This includes an array of environmentally friendly policies and practices at the federal, state, and city levels. Throughout American cities we see a push toward renewable energy, improved public transportation systems, green buildings, smaller homes, more parks and trees, bicycle lanes, and an improved culture of recycling our waste.

In addition to the sprouting of community gardens and farmers markets, which focus on the local production and consumption of organic foods, cities like New York and Los Angeles have launched ambitious green campaigns to plant 1 million trees and other policies to create greener cities. While all of these efforts represent a breath of fresh air, especially after eight years of anti-environmental policies and practices under the Bush administration, what is missing from this green movement is the credit deserved for those responsible to making cities like Los Angeles greener, cleaner, and more beautiful: Mexican immigrants.

More specifically, I'm referring to paid Mexican gardeners, or what I call green urban workers, who toil from dawn to dusk, seven days a week, mowing our lawns, creating attractive landscapes, planting our trees, and controlling pests.

Through their daily labor and creativity, Mexican gardeners help reduce pollution in cities and suburbs. In a 2005 article in *Environmental Management*, researchers found that green turfs (which includes front lawns and parks) provide an array of ecological benefits, such as slower storm runoff, improved water infiltration, and offset of what researchers refer to as the urban heat-island effect.

Moreover, by planting and maintaining urban trees, Mexican gardeners help reduce urban pollution. For example, apart from providing shade and beautifying the city, trees filter dust and pollutants, absorb carbon dioxide, release oxygen, and help with water runoff.

However, instead of receiving recognition for creating environmentally friendly and healthier places for the average American, Mexican gardeners and immigrants in general get little respect in this country. The popular portrayal of Mexican gardeners, for instance, frequently consists of negative stereotypes. This includes pejorative images and narratives found in Hollywood movies, newspapers, television, legislative bodies, and academic arenas, depicting Mexican gardeners, like Latina domestic workers, as ignorant, second-class citizens, public nuisances and, overall, objects of ridicule.

From C.N.N.'s recently departed Lou Dobbs to the late Samuel P. Huntington of Harvard, Mexican immigrants symbolize "social burdens" and "threats" to American society. Internalizing the prevailing negative stigma associated with so-called immigrant jobs, too often Latino actors complain about being typecast in "demeaning immigrant roles" as gardeners and domestic workers. Instead, Latino actors, along with civic leaders and others, should fight to have Hollywood create three-dimensional roles of hired gardeners and domestic workers as honest, hard-working individuals in this country, in lieu of the caricatures that we see on television and in movies.

We can also see the bashing of immigrants in this country during the current health-care debate. In his recent speech to a joint session of Congress, President Obama, when speaking about how undocumented immigrants will be excluded from his health-care reform plan, Congressman Joe Wilson (R-S.C.) shouted, "You lie!" for the world to hear. What a shame!

Now, bashing immigrants is not new in this country, since Americans have commonly blamed others for their problems, especially during times of crises. What continues to baffle me, however, is that immigrants work in the most dangerous and lowest-paid jobs in America, yet receive the least protection when it comes to abuse in the work place and work-related injuries.

In the case of Mexican gardeners, these workers not only put in long hours, but also work with dangerous machines and use chemicals that pose serious danger to their health. They also risk their lives when climbing trees without the proper tools and equipment commonly used by city workers. L.A. city workers, for example, can prune trees using an aerial lift found on city-owned trucks. Too many Mexican gardeners have died while trimming trees in Los Angeles and beyond so that we can breathe cleaner air.

It is time that we recognize these green urban workers for all of their positive contributions to making our cities greener, safer, and more beautiful, by providing them with the training, equipment, and health services that they require to do their jobs. While doing so, we need to recognize that when we speak about the greening of our cities, what we're also talking about is the browning of American cities. Thus, it's time that we provide these honest, hard-working people with the respect, dignity, and honor they deserve.

South Bend, IN, 2009

C.N.N. Must Drop Host Lou Dobbs for Stirring Anti-immigrant Hysteria

It's time for C.N.N. to drop Lou Dobbs, the extremist cable host, from its network for his constant assaults on immigrants and Latinos in this country. In contrast to C.N.N.'s balanced news anchors, Campbell Brown and Anderson Cooper, whose mantra is "Keeping Them Honest," Dobbs constantly spews his xenophobic views on a regular basis. Maybe the charismatic Cooper can do us all a favor by keeping Dobbs honest?

It's amazing to me how Dobbs blames immigrants, particularly Mexican immigrants, for everything that's wrong with this country. From crime to disease, from the recession to the so-called erosion of American values, according to Dobbs immigrants or what he calls "illegal aliens" appear to be the source of this country's problems.

While everyone has the right to his or her own opinions, not everyone has a right to his own facts. Dobbs claims, for example, that undocumented immigrants account for one-third of the total U.S. prison population. When journalist Amy Goodman of *Democracy Now!* questioned this figure, countering that only 6 percent of the total prison population consists of non-citizens (which includes undocumented immigrants and others), Dobbs appeared unfazed about reporting false information to support his views of immigrants.

In addition to crime, Dobbs constantly fabricates and exaggerates the role that undocumented immigrants play in the spread of disease in this country. Dobbs claims that immigrants pose a danger to this country by spreading diseases such as tuberculosis, malaria, and leprosy, without providing scientific research to support his claims. For example, Dobbs said that undocumented immigrants cause 7,000 cases of leprosy every three years in the U.S. Contradicting this claim, television journalist Lesley Stahl of "60 Minutes" found that only 7,000 cases of leprosy have been reported during past 30 years in the U.S., without any direct link to immigrants. When questioned by Stahl on "60 Minutes," Dobbs seemed unconcerned about the gross discrepancies between his statements and the facts.

When it comes to the economy, undocumented immigrants, according to Dobbs, have wreaked havoc on this country's financial stability. While it's one thing to blame corporate America for outsourcing jobs to foreign countries and to hold the federal government accountable for free-trade policies that endanger the middle-class in this country, it's quite another thing to hold undocumented immigrants responsible for America's economic ills. How in the world can an undocumented immigrant who works in a service-oriented job that most Americans avoid due to the low wages and social stigma associated with so-called immigrant jobs, present a threat to America's economic prosperity?

Instead of attacking Lehman Brothers and the Republicans' reckless deregulation policies for hurting the American economy, Dobbs and fellow conservatives act like it's the Garcia brothers and their willingness to work in this country's most dangerous and lowest-paying jobs that best explains the current economic meltdown.

Apart from linking undocumented immigrants to the United States' current problems related to crime, disease, and the recession, Dobbs and other conservatives assert that recent immigrants threaten the social fabric of this country. For example, the late political scientist Samuel Huntington of Harvard University famously wrote an essay titled "The Hispanic Challenge," where the distinguished professor unabashedly portrayed Mexican immigration in particular as one of the biggest threats to the "Anglo-Protestant values that built the American dream." It's maddening to see that, in a time when many people claim that we live in a so-called post-racial society, especially with the election of Barack Obama to the presidency and successful appointment of Sonia Sotomayor as Supreme Court justice, that powerful public figures like Huntington and Dobbs can spew their anti-immigrant views without internal pressures from reputable institutions like Harvard and C.N.N., respectively.

Shame on them all.

As with the Civil Rights Movement for the black community, it's incumbent upon the growing Latino community, especially those of Mexican descent, along with individuals who value a society free of discrimination and exploitation, to help remove Dobbs from his privileged position at C.N.N. C.N.N. is not a public or democratically elected institution, where we have a constitutional right to vote for who speaks on behalf of this organization. We can, however, put pressure by boycotting the corporations that underwrite Dobbs' anti-immigrant views through advertisement dollars. Those corporations whose advertisement dollars keep Dobbs on the air are guilty by association and don't deserve the tremendous purchasing power of the Latino community.

Fortunately, an ongoing effort led by community leaders and a coalition of pro-immigrant advocacy groups, such as bastadobbs.com, are currently engaged in a campaign to stop Dobbs from spreading more hate and fear against honest, hard-working people in this country. In short, the time has come for those who believe in a more just and humane society to work together toward sending Lou Dobbs to where he belongs: Fox News.

{editor's note: Lou Dobbs was forced to resign from CNN on November 11, 2009}

My Mexican Immigrant Parents Died
Due to Lack of Health Care

The American government, in my opinion, contributed to the deaths of my parents by not providing universal health care. In every other advanced industrial nation, they would have received quality health care as a right. Here they did not.

My father first came to this country as an agricultural worker from Mexico during the Bracero Program, and he and my mother settled in the United States legally, with work permits, in the late 1960s. He later worked dead-end jobs in different factories while my mother labored as a domestic worker—cleaning the homes of countless middle-class Americans—for more than 40 years. Neither of them accumulated enough wealth to afford a home of their own for my siblings and me, much less afford private health care.

My father died in 1996 after a prolonged battle with prostate cancer. My mother died earlier this year after a major stroke left her bedridden for many months. If only my father and mother had had access to government-supported health care before the symptoms of prostate cancer and heart problems reached a critical stage, they might have lived many years longer.

Most doctors will tell a patient, for example, that with regular checkups, proper diet, medications, and exercise, severe medical conditions such as prostate cancer and heart complications can be treatable. But they couldn't afford the regular checkups that could have extended their lives.

We need universal health care in this country, or at the very least a public option that will cover the 47 million Americans without coverage today. Isn't it hypocritical that the conservatives in Congress who ferociously attack the public option themselves benefit from a public option? As taxpayers, we not only pay their salaries but we also provide them with a health-care insurance plan they can access, and if they are seniors or veterans, they're already covered by a public option that works well: Medicare or Veterans Affairs.

It makes no sense for President Obama and Democrats in Congress to reach a bipartisan agreement with a conservative party that is beholden to special interests—the existing private health-care industry—and that is diametrically opposed to domestic government programs that benefit the public. At the end of the day, any bill that excludes a public option would represent just another case of corporate power prevailing over the public interest, of Wall Street conquering Main Street. Once again, the less fortunate would lose out to people of privilege, who could afford the skyrocketing costs of premiums, co-pays, and deductibles. It was just these costs that my parents couldn't cover—and they paid with their lives. Now, my 10-year-old son, Joaquin, has no paternal grandparents. He misses them. So does my wife, Antonia, and so do I.

Los Angeles, CA, 2009

Immigration: The Elephant in the Room

Where's Barak Obama's speech on immigration? Not that I want to place one more burden on the Illinois senator and presidential candidate—he's already been unjustifiably challenged to account for the remnants of racism in the United States. But is there no one else with or without a Spanish surname to deliver an equally powerful discourse about the positive contributions immigrants make to this country?

There's nothing like a presidential election to raise the volume on the xenophobic rhetoric of anti-immigration diehards. Television talk-show hosts and politicians quickly jump at the opportunity to bash Mexican immigrants like a piñata at a kid's birthday party. These same voices suffer from selective amnesia, purposely forgetting the immense contributions of Mexican immigrants, focusing instead on the "costs" associated with our presence here.

As the son of Mexican immigrants who lacked formal education, I often ask myself, "What about the costs that immigrants incur to come here?" I have been pondering this question a lot since my recent migration from U.C.L.A. to U.C. Berkeley to pursue my doctoral studies in the Department of City and Regional Planning. In temporarily leaving my wife, Antonia Montes, and 8-year-old son behind in Los Angeles, I can't help but feel I'm following in the footsteps of my immigrant father, who came to *El Norte* more than half a century ago to pick fruits and vegetables as part of the U.S.-Mexico guest-worker plan, the Bracero Program.

Although being a doctoral student at a prestigious university cannot compare with being a farm worker—or, indeed, a domestic worker like my mother—it gives me some idea of how my father felt. The sacrifices I'm now making, while temporary, seem very real to me. I worry about how my wife will manage to keep her teaching job while attending graduate school and caring for our son. Will she be able to take him to his piano lessons or chess tournaments? Will I be able to make his third-grade parent conference? How can I focus on Foucault while my son cries himself to sleep because I'm not there to kiss him goodnight?

Yet I want to be careful not to overstate the similarities, given that immigrants like my parents faced much harsher challenges. After all, between 1942 and 1964, the Bracero Program provided jobs to hundreds of thousands of Mexican workers, including my grandfather, father, and uncles, most of whom lived in substandard housing, worked long hours under terrible conditions for poor wages, and experienced racism and abuse from American employers and local citizens. Unlike them, however, I know that my son will have infinite opportunities in his life.

What troubles me is the fate of the 11 million-plus undocumented immigrants and their children who are in this country. Will their hard labor and daily sacrifice produce long-term payoffs for themselves and their offspring?

Will mowing lawns, taking care of other people's children, picking fruit, and hand-washing S.U.V.s in West L.A. help them accumulate enough wealth to get ahead? Will they be able to purchase a home some day on (sub)minimum wages or establish enough financial and human capital to send their children to the world's top public universities?

South Bend, IN, 2009

Migrating to El Norte

When things go bad, many Americans commonly blame someone else for their problems. Historically, immigrants have been convenient scapegoats: they not only "take away" jobs from "hard-working" American citizens and deplete the country's resources, the argument goes, but they are criminals who have entered this country illegally and must be punished with jail or deportation.

There is nothing like a presidential election to raise the volume on this xenophobic rhetoric. Television talk-show hosts and politicians quickly jump at the opportunity to bash Mexican immigrants like a piñata at a kid's birthday party, especially in a time of political and economic crisis. These same voices suffer from selective amnesia, purposely forgetting the contributions Mexican immigrants have made to this country, both historically and in the present, and focusing instead on the "costs" associated with our presence here.

As the son of Mexican immigrants, I commonly ask myself, "What about the costs that immigrants incur to come here?" I find myself pondering this basic question even more frequently lately, since I recently migrated here to pursue my doctoral studies in the Department of City and Regional Planning, temporarily leaving my wife, Antonia Montes, and 8-year-old son, Joaquin, behind in Los Angeles.

While such arrangements are made regularly by graduate students everywhere, regardless of their ethnicity or citizenship status, I can't help but feel as though, in a meaningful way, I'm following in the footsteps of my immigrant father, who came to *El Norte* more than half a century ago to pick fruits and vegetables as part of the U.S.-Mexico guest-worker plan, the Bracero Program.

Although being a doctoral student cannot compare to being a farm worker (or domestic worker, like my mother), it gives me some idea of how my father felt when he, like many other Mexican immigrants, left his community and family to work in *El Norte*. The sacrifices I'm now making, while temporary, seem very real to me: I worry about how my wife will manage to keep her teaching job and attend graduate school herself while caring for our son. Will she be able to take him to his chess tournaments? What about baseball season? Can she volunteer at the snack stand and see him hit a home run at the same time? Will I be able to make his third-grade parent conference?

Yet I want to be careful not to overstate the similarities, for those immigrants faced much harsher challenges than I face today. Between 1942 and 1964, the Bracero Program provided the U.S. with hundreds of thousands of Mexican workers as a way to meet the labor shortages of World War II and beyond.

By 1945, more than 62,000 Mexican immigrants were working in the railroad industry while another 58,000 toiled as agricultural laborers, among them my grandfather, father, and uncles. These workers, for the most part, lived in substandard housing, worked long hours under terrible conditions for poor wages, and experienced racism and abuse from American employers and local citizens.

Things haven't changed much in a half-century for many Mexican immigrants in this country. Too often they continue to live in substandard conditions, work at the most difficult jobs for long hours, and experience employer harassment on a regular basis. The predicament of undocumented immigrants is even more precarious, since many do not report work-related cases of abuse. In many cases, undocumented immigrants do not go to the police or a hospital during an emergency because they fear they may face deportation. This is hardly fair compensation for the many sacrifices many Mexican immigrants make to come to this country, beginning with their efforts to save or borrow enough money to cross the treacherous U.S.-Mexico border.

When I think about the challenges that millions of undocumented workers make to get by in this country, I realize that I'm in a privileged situation: I'm giving up an office job to return to graduate school, not bidding my family goodbye for months or years while I struggle to make enough money to send back to them. Whereas the undocumented come north with only the desperate hope of a better life, I know that my own sacrifices will almost certainly pay off in the future, as I and my wife both secure positions in academia, giving my son more opportunities than I had growing up in East Los Angeles' Ramona Gardens housing project.

Mexican immigrants leave their families behind without knowing when they'll see them again. It's amazing what many of them will tolerate in order to survive in such a hostile environment, confronted for the most part by only the bleakest opportunities. What will it take for their offspring to attend a university?

Striking Out in Phoenix: M.L.B.'s
Lack of Respect for Latinos

Major League Baseball Commissioner Bud Selig recently struck out, big time, by stubbornly refusing to relocate the 82nd All-Star Game from Phoenix, Arizona, to another city due to the desert state's racist immigration law, SB 1070. Although the core of this harsh law remains under a federal court injunction, if Arizona Governor Jan Brewer has her way, it can go all the way to the conservative-dominated Supreme Court and set a devastating legal precedent against 50 million Latinos in the U.S.

Numerous civil-rights and immigrant advocate groups have taken a moral and financial position against a law that promotes racial profiling of all Latinos, especially since SB 1070 allows for police officers and other government officials to demand legal documents from individuals under the guise of "reasonable suspicion." The fundamental problem here is that those most likely to be targeted will be brown-skinned individuals and those with Spanish-surnames. Despite this fact, Selig and the owners of the major league baseball teams don't care that almost 30% of the M.L.B. baseball players—those of Latin American descent with Spanish surnames like Gonzalez, Rivera, and Rodriguez—will be directly impacted by this racist law that has spread like wildfire to other states, such as Utah, Indiana, South Carolina, Georgia, and Alabama.

Taking the so-called apolitical position that America's greatest pastime will not get involved in a law that should be settled through the political process, Selig conveniently ignores the fact that locating the All-Star Game in Phoenix in the first place represents a political act. It's no secret that m

Major U.S. cities compete against one another to secure the next major sports event, such as the National Football League Super Bowl, National Basketball Association All-Star Game, and major international events. Not only do governors and mayors get involved in this competitive process on behalf of their states and cities to capture the financial and publicity benefits of major professional games, but so also do key business interests that benefit directly from those individuals and families who purchase tickets, consume food, drink alcohol, rent hotels, attend tourist attractions, and buy memorabilia.

This is not the first time that the Latino community has been taken for granted by major league baseball. In the mid-1900s, for example, then-Brooklyn Dodgers owner Walter O'Malley and his friends had no problem in displacing an entire Latino community, Chavez Ravine, to make room for the new tenants: the Los Angeles Dodgers.

By labeling the barrio as "blighted," the Housing Authority of Los Angeles in cahoots with the federal government utilized eminent domain—the legal practice of taking private property from individuals for the common good—to forcefully clear the land of its long-time residents. While originally intended for public housing projects, O'Malley and his power friends in City Hall eventually prevailed by locating a professional baseball team in a major market like Los Angeles. To the present, living family members who lost their homes vividly remember this tragic American story.

Despite this dark history, Latino fans continue to wear Dodger blue, spend their hard-earned money on tickets, parking, over-priced beer, and Dodger Dogs, and what do the Latino baseball fans get in return for their loyalty? A dysfunctional owner, Frank McCourt, and an insensitive commissioner, who refuses to meet one simple demand from Latino and Latina leaders: to relocate a major league baseball game to another state on the basic premise that we, as a society, can't reward states racist and inhospitable against Latinos.

Is this too much to ask? Didn't the N.F.L. relocate the Super Bowl in 1993 from Phoenix to Pasadena, California, since this same desert state refused to recognize Dr. Martin Luther King, Jr. Day as a paid holiday?

How can the M.L.B. continue to boast about being a leader in the civil-rights movement with the historic case of Jackie Robinson—the first great African American baseball ball player in 1947 to break the dehumanizing color line—when it ignores Arizona's institutional racism against Latinos in general and immigrants in particular?

While it's too late for the M.L.B. to reverse its course on the recently played All-Star Game at Chase Field on July 12, 2011, it's not too late for the millions of Latino baseball fans in this country to sit on the bench, permanently, when the next baseball game takes place in any field. Instead of pleading for change, Latinos need to learn from the brave African American men and woman who refused to take the bus in Montgomery, Alabama, on December 1, 1955, until they received the dignity and respect that they deserved.

South Bend, IN, 2009

Seeing How the Other Half Lives:
The Working Poor and Immigrants

In times of financial turmoil and massive corporate bailouts, we shouldn't forget one simple fact: the working poor in this country have historically been marginalized and blamed for their impoverished status. This has been especially true for racial minorities and immigrants in the nation's ghettoes and barrios since as long ago as the nineteenth century.

Immigrants and the working poor are no strangers to housing instability, high job loss and unemployment, tight credit markets, lack of health coverage, and other social and economic ills currently plaguing millions of Americans. Why is it that only when economic downturns hit the middle and upper classes that America finds itself in desperate need of trillion-dollar federal interventions?

Throughout its history, America has blamed the working poor and its most recent wave of immigrants for their low socio-economic status. If only they learned the virtues of the so-called Protestant work ethic, the logic goes, "those people" would succeed in America, the famed land of opportunity. If only "those immigrants" learned to speak proper English and adopt America's cultural norms of individualism, hard work, and self-motivation, goes the xenophobic argument, they would become productive members of society.

This is not to say that government intervention hasn't addressed the needs of the working poor.

F.D.R.'s New Deal and Johnson's Great Society programs provided the working poor with vital monetary aid and services in employment, health care, and education. Despite the good intentions behind many liberal government programs and services, however, mainstream and conservative voices have stigmatized anti-poverty programs and services as handouts for "lazy, undeserving individuals" who represent, in economists' terms, free riders.

As someone who grew up in East L.A. housing projects on welfare, food stamps, and free school meals and medical services, I'm all too familiar with the social stigma associated with these government benefits. Although most of my childhood friends in the Ramona Gardens housing project also received food stamps, using them at the local store typically made us feel like drug addicts buying heroine in a dark alley.

The stigma of being poor was another source of exasperation for many of us when we participated in a mandatory busing program to a majority-white school, Mt. Gleason Jr. High, in Sunland Tujunga in the late 1970s. Despite the obvious fact that we "dressed poor" and received free school meals compared to the mostly affluent white students, I never heard anyone from our barrio admit to being poor or on welfare. For us, this would have been tantamount to admitting to a heinous crime, such as, say, waterboarding.

This stigma continued through my undergraduate years at U.C.L.A. in the mid-1980s. When filling out my financial-aid application, for example, my household income consisted of a meager $8,000. This for a family of eight, not to mention the fact that welfare doesn't technically count as income—it's government aid, after all. But I kept this simple fact a secret from my U.C.L.A. peers, who came mostly from stable, middle-class backgrounds.

In fact, it wasn't until I studied U.S. history that I learned I had nothing to be ashamed of and that the working poor have contributed greatly to making America the most wealthy and powerful country in the world. Yet, in contrast to anti-poverty policies, government programs and services aimed at boosting the middle and upper classes, such as the G.I. Bill, mortgage-interest tax deductions for homeowners, and the recent Bush administration tax cuts for the rich have hardly received the same stigma and public scorn. While it's true that many government intervention programs and subsidies, together with access to higher education, home ownership, and tax breaks have helped create a significant middle class, whites have been the main beneficiaries of these policies as they fled from inner cities to the suburbs.

In short, there seems to be a double standard in government interventions aimed at helping Americans. Whereas government aid to the working poor is pregnant with social stigmas and attacks by conservatives, aid that addresses the needs of the higher classes, including victims of financial fallouts, is perceived as perfectly normal. While recessions impact all people, not all people suffer equally.

For the majority of the working poor, a bad economy is one more crisis to deal with on a daily basis, while the upper classes get a taste of what it feels like to live at the bottom: insecurity, anxiety, and a pervasive sense of gloom. But if every crisis has a silver lining, my hope is that this time around, privileged Americans and government officials alike will have more compassion for the less fortunate instead of scapegoating them for the nation's ills.

Brick by Brick: Ode to My Mexican Mother

My mother built her own home, brick by brick. Too poor to get a piece of the American Dream, at 50 years of age, while still living in East Los Angeles' Ramona Gardens housing project, she decided to build her own home in Tijuana, Mexico. When she told my siblings and me—all eight of us—of her plans, we all thought she had gone mad.

"What are you going to do over there all by yourself?" I asked.

"Don't worry," she told me in Spanish. "I'm going to build a room for each one of you."

Our family, like many families of Mexican origin, has a strong bond with Tijuana—a place where countless immigrants first settle before making their arduous journey to *el norte*. My parents first migrated to this border city from a *rancho* in Michoacán, fleeing a bloody family feud that claimed the life of my uncle Pascual. Like a "good wife," my mother relocated with my father and his siblings—all nine of them—to the hillsides of this poor yet vibrant city. Unlike the U.S., the poor in Latin America, for the most part, live on the hillsides while the affluent reside in the city core.

Once settled in Tijuana, she managed to get a work visa in San Diego as a *doméstica* (domestic worker), cleaning the homes of mainly white, middle-class families, while she left her young children at home. In her absence, my older sisters took on the "mother" role by cleaning, cooking and caring for the younger ones.

Not one to conform, my mother, during her fifth pregnancy, arranged for me to be born in *los estados unidos*. Accessing her kinship networks in the U.S., I was born in Sacramento. Isn't San Diego closer to the border? Regardless of this mystery, having a U.S.-born child facilitated the process for my family to successfully apply for *micas* (green cards) in this country. While Republicans refer to individuals like myself as "anchor babies," I reject this pejorative label.

Once in the U.S., my mother continued to labor as a *doméstica* while my father earned minimum wage in dead-end jobs. Due to their lack of formal education and non-existent English skills, accompanied by low-occupational skills, my parents eventually applied for public housing assistance in East Los Angeles. After raising her children in an environment plagued by abject poverty, violence, drugs, gangs, police abuse, and bleak prospects associated with inner-city housing projects, my mother decided to return to the motherland—Mexico—to pursue her dreams.

During my freshman year at U.C.L.A., my mother phoned me about her ambitious plan: she had bought a small empty lot in Tijuana to build her dream home. While initially shocked, I asked for an emergency student loan to help her with this goal. If the financial-aid office had asked me at the time to justify the loan, I probably would've said something like, "Help mother escape from projects."

Not long after acquiring the land, my mother gave my siblings and me a tour of her new purchase. Like a recent architecture graduate from U.C. Berkeley embarking on a major design project, she created a visual image of her plans for us.

"This is where the kitchen will go, and over there I'll build the living room," she told us on our first visit, as we surveyed the uneven, dirt-filled lot. Without saying a word, we all looked at one another, wondering if she could pull it off.

In retrospect, we should've never doubted her. This is the same woman, who at 13 years of age, hit a menacing man in the head with a rock, as he failed to kidnap her on the *rancho*. Had he kidnapped her for several days and then returned her home, she would have been forced to marry her abductor to "save her honor," a barbaric practice that continues to the present throughout the world. This is the same woman who worked as a *doméstica* in the U.S. for over 40 years to provide for her family, who "forced" my father to take my brother and me—as lazy teenagers—to Malibu as *jornaleros* (day laborers) so that we could appreciate the importance of a college education.

"If you don't take them to work," she threatened my father, as he watched *Bonanza* re-runs, "then I'll take them myself." For over 10 years, my mother, with the help of my sisters, slowly built her dream house, brick by brick. First came the cement foundation, then the walls, followed by the roof. Then came the windows and doors. Not satisfied with a one-story house, she eventually built a two-story home, with a detached guest house in the back.

Defying the odds, she transformed an empty lot of land, filled with rocks, used tires, and broken glass into the most beautiful house on the block. She hired and fired workers, fixed leaky faucets and remodeled, painted and repainted like there was no end.

For me, this house became my mother's obsession, but for my mother, it symbolized her true passion, to create something out of nothing, and she wasn't going to let anyone jeopardize her dream. I only wish she could have lived one more day so that she could buy that magenta bed comforter from downtown Los Angeles that she was looking for.

Photo by Ed Carreon

Alvaro Huerta

Alvaro Huerta is an urban planning scholar, nationally syndicated writer, and public intellectual. Currently, he's a Visiting Scholar at U.C.L.A.'s Chicano Studies Research Center. He has published widely in academic journals, magazines, newspapers, book anthologies, encyclopedias, and online outlets. He earned advanced degrees from the two flagship campuses of the prestigious University of California, a B.A. in history and M.A. in urban planning from U.C.L.A. and a Ph.D. in city and regional planning from U.C. Berkeley. As a social scientist, Dr. Huerta's research interests include the following academic fields: urban planning, social network analysis, immigration, social movements, Chicana/o history, Latina/o politics, and the informal economy. Completed in the fall of 2011, his dissertation focuses on Mexican immigrants and their social networks in Los Angeles' informal economy. The title is: "Examining the Perils and Promises of an Informal Niche in a Global City: A Case Study of Mexican Immigrant Gardeners in Los Angeles."

Raised in East Los Angeles' notorious Ramona Gardens housing project (better known as the Big Hazard projects) and the product of inner-city public schools, Dr. Huerta is happily married to his wonderful wife, Antonia Montes. He is the son of Mexican immigrants, Salomón Chavez Huerta, Sr. and Carmen Mejia Huerta, from a small rancho, *Sajo Grande*, in Michoacán.

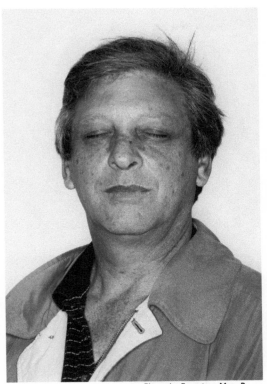
Photo by Francisco Mata Rosas

Antonio Turok, Photographer

Antonio Turok, born In Mexico City in 1955, is an internationally known documentary photographer who has worked in Central America, Mexico, and the United States for the last 35 years covering the human condition of the people of Mexico.

Mr. Turok is a recipient of the following grants: National Institute of Fine Arts (I.N.B.A.), Maine Photographic Workshop Book Award, 1994 Mother Jones International Fund for Documentary Photography Award, John Simon Guggenheim Foundation and the U.S.A.-Mexico Fund for Culture Rockefeller / Bancomer Award, and The F.O.N.C.A.-National System Award for Artists in Mexico. He has published two books, *Imágenes de Nicaragua* (Casa de Las Imágenes, 1988) and *Chiapas: End of Silence* (Aperture, 1998). His work has been collected by numerous museums in Mexico, Europe, and the United States: the Los Angeles County Museum of Fine Arts, the Museum of Mexican Art in Chicago, the Wittliff Gallery of Mexican and Southwestern Photography, San Marcos, Texas, and many more.

Mr. Turok lives and teaches in Oaxaca, Mexico.